Quiet Time

Octopus schedules
 strangle us.
  Escalating details,
   dema... ... ...
    the s
     suff
Oh, to b
 rocked
  freed
   in th
It takes a
 Special Friend
  to give such an embrace ...
   One who said
    "Come unto Me
     all you who labour and are
      heavy laden,
       and I will give you rest."
One called
 Jesus.
  Rest in Him.

FROM 'EVERYBODY'S BREAKING PIECES OFF OF ME!'
BY SUSAN L. LENZKES, DISCOVERY HOUSE PUBLISHERS. COPYRIGHT© 1992.

GW00715414

*"Search me, O God, and know
my heart; test me and know
my anxious thoughts."*

PSALM 139:23

THE CAUSE – THE CURE

No two people react to stress in quite the same way. One person may revel in frequent change, while another may be thrown into a state of disquiet at the slightest change in their lives and life style.

Take time alone in the presence of God and ask Him to help you identify the causes of your stress. God wants to teach you how to respond to life so that, instead of a breakdown, you experience a breakthrough into a new way of living.

❖

"Do not be anxious about any-thing, but in everything ... present your requests to God."

PHILIPPIANS 4:6

THE RIGHT DIRECTION

God wants to sharpen your ability to recognise the things that contribute to stress in your life, so that all your energies can be channelled in the right way.

He will teach you how to turn your weaknesses into strengths, and how to handle your stress. Even if you cannot change your surroundings, He will help you to change your perceptions so that, instead of being immersed in self-activity, your energy will be directed into spiritual activity.

*"There is a time for
everything ..."*

ECCLESIASTES 3:1

ALL THE TIME IN THE WORLD

I t is all too easy in the rush and whirl of modern life to become a slave to the clock. God wants to save us from being obsessed by time and placing ourselves under unnecessary stress. We may be in a hurry, but God isn't.

Learn the wisdom of letting things develop at their own pace. Relax and do not become intimidated by time. You have all the time in the world to do the things that God wants you to do.

❖

God can take a person overcome by stress, and build into their lives insights and principles which will enable them to live above and beyond its paralysing grip. With God all things are possible.

If we work in obedience to His promptings, Christ can help us to adjust our life style and 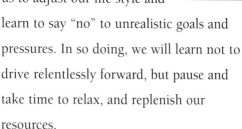 learn to say "no" to unrealistic goals and pressures. In so doing, we will learn not to drive relentlessly forward, but pause and take time to relax, and replenish our resources.

❖

"See how the lilies of the field grow. They do not labour or spin."

MATTHEW 6:28

CWR CWR Waverley Abbey House, Waverley Lane,
Farnham, Surrey GU9 8EP

National Distributors

AUSTRALIA: Christian Marketing Pty Ltd Tel: (052) 413 288
CANADA: CMC Distribution Ltd Tel: 1-800-325-1297
MALAYSIA: Salvation Book Centre (M) Tel: (3) 7766411
NEW ZEALAND: Christian Marketing NZ Ltd Tel: 0508 535659 (toll free)
NIGERIA: FBFM Tel: (01) 611 160
REPUBLIC OF IRELAND: Scripture Union Tel: (01) 8363764
SINGAPORE: Alby Commercial Ent Pte. Ltd Tel: (65) 741 0411
SOUTH AFRICA: Struik Christian Books (Pty Ltd)   Tel: (021) 551 5900
USA: CMC Distribution Tel: 1-800-325-1297

❖

EVERY DAY
with Jesus

ISBN 1-85345-086-3

9 781853 450860

sufficient

Grace

❖